First Facts®

Amazing Animal Architects

≫ AMAZING ≪ Animal Architects on Land

A 4D BOOK

by Rebecca Rissman

Consultants:
James L. Gould
Professor
Department of Ecology and Evolutionary Biology
Princeton University

Carol Grant Gould
Science Writer
Princeton, N.J.

PEBBLE
a capstone imprint

Download the Capstone 4D app!

- Ask an adult to download the Capstone 4D app.

- Scan the cover and stars inside the book for additional content.

When you scan a spread, you'll find fun extra stuff to go with this book! You can also find these things on the web at www.capstone4D.com using the password: land.26844

First Facts are published by Pebble
1710 Roe Crest Drive, North Mankato, Minnesota 56003
www.mycapstone.com

Library of Congress Cataloging-in-Publication Data
Names: Rissman, Rebecca, author.
Title: Amazing animal architects on land : A 4D book /
   by Rebecca Rissman.
Description: North Mankato, Minnesota : an imprint of Pebble, [2019] |
   Series: First facts. Amazing animal architects | "Pebble is published by
   Capstone." | Audience: Ages 6–8. | Includes index.
Identifiers: LCCN 2017057842 (print) | LCCN 2018005881 (ebook) | ISBN
   9781543526929 (ebook PDF) | ISBN 9781543526844 (hardcover) | ISBN
   9781543526882 (pbk.)
Subjects: LCSH: Animals—Habitations—Juvenile literature. | Animal
   behavior—Juvenile literature.
Classification: LCC QL756 (ebook) | LCC QL756 .R56 2018 (print) | DDC
   591.56/4—dc23
LC record available at https://lccn.loc.gov/2017057842ç

Editorial Credits
Karen Aleo, editor; Sarah Bennett, designer; Morgan Walters, media researcher;
Tori Abraham, production specialist

Photo Credits
Alamy: Nature Picture Library, 11; Getty Images: Anthony Mercieca, 15, Auscape /UIG, 21, James H Robinson, 17, Norbert Rosing, 13, Thomas Marent/ Minden Pictures, 7; Newscom: Horst Mahr imageBROKER, 9; Shutterstock: Chutima Chaochaiya, (blueprint) design element, John Carnemolla, 5, Miloje, (grunge) design element, Natalia5988, (brush grunge) design element, Pavel Krasensky, 6, Peter Hermes Furian, (map) design element, Sergey Uryadnikov, cover; Wikimedia: Zoë Helene Kindermann, 19

Printed in China.
000306

Table of Contents

Busy Builders

Animal architects are busy! They build giant mounds, tiny huts, and icy **dens**. They make these homes or nests on land for many reasons. These places keep animals safe from harsh weather. They can also provide a safe place to raise young. And some help attract a **mate**.

den—a place where a wild animal may live
mate—the male or female partner in a pair of animals; mates join together to produce young.

Great bowerbird males build to attract a mate.

Wood Ants

What's that giant mound? It's a wood ant nest! Wood ants work together to build enormous homes. They often cover an old tree stump in sticks, pine needles, and other materials. This becomes their mound.

Inside the mound, ants make tunnels and rooms. Some rooms are used to store food. Others are used to raise young.

Polar Bears

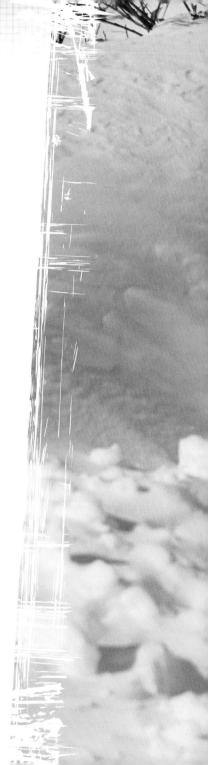

Scrape! Scratch! In the fall or winter, a pregnant polar bear digs into the snow. She makes a small tunnel and lies down inside. More snow falls and seals the den shut.

The den is a safe place for the polar bear to give birth. It protects the cubs from **predators** and cold weather. The bears stay inside until spring.

predator—an animal that hunts other animals for food

WHERE POLAR BEARS LIVE
Polar bear dens are found in deep snowdrifts.

RANGE MAP

Western Meadowlarks

Western meadowlarks build sturdy and safe nests. A female bird uses her beak to make a hole in the soil. Then she gathers dry grasses, stems, and pieces of bark. She makes a bowl-shaped nest. Some birds stop here. Others keep building. They make **domed** roofs over their nests. These nests shelter the bird's eggs.

FACT

Some western meadowlarks build their nests on top of dried cow footprints.

WHERE HAZEL DORMICE LIVE
In winter, dormouse nests are found under leaf piles or near logs.

RANGE MAP

Malleefowl

Malleefowl build warm nests. They lay their eggs on a bed of wet leaves and sand. Then they bury the eggs in more sand. The rotting leaves create heat. Sand keeps the heat inside. This keeps the eggs warm until they hatch.

FACT

Male malleefowl keep their nests the right **temperature**. If the eggs get too cold, males add sand to the nest. If the eggs get too hot, they move sand away.

temperature—the measure of how hot or cold something is

WHERE MALLEEFOWL LIVE

These giant mounds are found on sandy ground in woodlands or shrublands.

RANGE MAP

Glossary

camouflage (KA-muh-flahzh)—to be made to blend in with the things around it

compass (KUHM-puhs)—an instrument used for finding directions

den (DEN)—a place where a wild animal may live

domed (DOHMD)—rounded on top

funnel (FUHN-uhl)—a wide tube that becomes narrow at the center

hibernate (HYE-bur-nate)—to spend winter in a deep sleep; animals hibernate to survive low temperatures and lack of food.

mate (MATE)—the male or female partner in a pair of animals; mates join together to produce young.

predator (PRED-uh-tur)—an animal that hunts other animals for food

saliva (suh-LYE-vuh)—the liquid in the mouth

silk (SILK)—a thin but strong thread made by spiders

temperature (TEM-pur-uh-chur)—the measure of how hot or cold something is

Read More

De Nijs, Erika. *A Spider's Web.* Animal Builders. New York: Cavendish Square Publishing, 2017.

Franchino, Vicky. *Animal Architects.* True Books: Amazing Animals. New York: Children's Press, 2016.

Marsh, Laura F. *Polar Bears.* National Geographic Kids. Washington, D.C.: National Geographic, 2013.

Internet Sites

Use FactHound to find Internet sites related to this book.

Visit *www.facthound.com*

Just type in 9781543526844 and go.

 Check out projects, games, and lots more at
www.capstonekids.com

Critical Thinking Questions

1. Explain three reasons why animals build nests, dens, or webs.

2. Some very small animals are able to build huge homes or nests. Explain how they can do this.

3. Which animals are able to control the temperature of their homes or nests? How do they do it?

Index